Megan Webster & Libby Castañón

Crosstalk

Communication tasks and games for students of
English at the pre-intermediate level

Student's Book 2

Oxford University Press

The authors would like to thank the teachers at the Southern Branch of the Anglo-Mexican Institute in Mexico City, who so willingly piloted the material for *Crosstalk* and provided valuable comments for the series.

Illustrations by David Till, Anne Morrow, Carl Keighley, Pam Stephens

Photographs by Lance Browne, Vernon Brooke

We are grateful to the following organizations for their help with photographs:
Associated Press Ltd., Birds Eye Foods Ltd., Centrehurst Ltd., Bruce Coleman Ltd., Daily Telegraph Colour Library, John Hillelson Agency Ltd. (Photo by Burt Glinn), Eric Hosking, ITT Consumer Products, Punch Publications Ltd., Scottish Tourist Board, Sunday Express, The Sunday Times London, Texas Instruments, Thames Valley Police.

Contents

Introduction

To the teacher

Book Two provides ideas and material for conversation practice at the pre-intermediate stage of language learning. Its principal aim is to bridge the gap between the language lesson and real world encounters in the target language through spontaneous use of language in natural or simulated situations. It is meant to be used as a regular supplement to the textbook when the student has learnt the structures needed for a given session. These structures are listed in the Teacher's Book to guide the teacher in his choice at different stages of the syllabus.

The amount of conversation which a student can sustain depends largely on the number of structures he has acquired. Thus a brief period of conversation may be anticipated in the first session, and a gradual lengthening of the conversation span as the student's linguistic resources increase. If conversation practice is instituted early and given regularly in the course, the student will gain an operational command of language at each level of learning which will gradually lead to fluency and accuracy.

The re-use of language items, which is the concern of every conscientious teacher, is implicit in conversation. Moreover, the satisfaction experienced by the student on being able to respond or voice his ideas in the target language will increase his motivation to learn.

To the student

This book is meant for students who are anxious to speak the language in a natural way while they are learning it. It is designed for adolescent and adult beginners, and is particularly useful for those working towards examinations with an oral compcnent such as the Cambridge First Certificate in English, as it demands constant use of the basic structures and provides practice of a wide range of everyday vocabulary and expressions.

Description of the course

The course comprises three books for the elementary, pre-intermediate and intermediate levels respectively. There are twenty structured sessions in each book. The sessions have a stimulus to generate open class discussion and a transfer. The latter may take the form of small group discussion, role playing, problem solving or a game.

Each book has an accompanying cassette of dialogues and passages. The purpose of the tapes is twofold: to expose the student to a variety of language and voices, and provide a situation to stimulate conversation.

The Teacher's Book contains clear guidelines in methodology, a list of the essential structures, tapescripts, and examples of the kind of conversation which can be expected in each session. The Teacher's Book, which covers all three of the students' books in the series, is an integral part of the course and will be particularly helpful for those teachers who know the value of conversation practice, but are apprehensive about 'letting their students go', so to speak, at the early stages of language learning.

Although the sessions are roughly structured to follow a standard basic language syllabus, the teacher need not of course work through the book, but can pick and choose according to the needs and interests of the class. He should also be ready to adapt the ideas in the book to meet the interests of his particular group. There is considerable variation of stimulus and transfer in order to attract and hold the student's attention. In addition, the course seeks to maintain a reasonable level of cultural and educational content.

1 Starting a conversation

A Open class discussion

1 Erika and Steve are on the deck of a cross channel ferry. Describe them. Say what they're wearing and what they have with them. Can you tell what the weather's like?

2 Erika and Steve don't know each other. However, Steve would like to talk to Erika. What do you think he's going to say to start a conversation with her?

Here are some ways of starting a conversation with a stranger:

Lovely/awful day, isn't it?
Excuse me. What time is it?
Cold/hot/windy/noisy, isn't it?
Do you mind if I open/close the window?
Is this seat taken?
Do you mind if I smoke?

3 The conversation between the two young people is on the tape. Listen to it and say:

how Steve begins the conversation
where Erika and Steve are going, and why
where they're from
what they do
what Steve says at the end of the conversation

B Role playing — in pairs

Roles: Two people on a train. They don't know each other. One starts up a conversation with the other.

They talk about: where they're going and why, where they're from, what they do, and, perhaps, their interests.

C Getting to know your classmates

Now, start a conversation with someone in your class. Find out where they're from, what they do, why they're studying English, etc.

Here are some more conversation starters for you:

Nice/interesting/boring class, isn't it?
English is hard, isn't it?
Excuse me, what's the name of that book?
The teacher speaks very fast, doesn't he?

2 Did you know?

A Open class discussion

1 Do you know which type of butterfly this is? It is black and orange with white spots.

2 Look at the map and guess what's special about this type of butterfly.

3 Listen to the tape and note down:

a The butterfly's name
b How long it lives
c Where it lives in the summer
d Where it migrates to
e How far it can travel

4 Now tell the class about this butterfly.

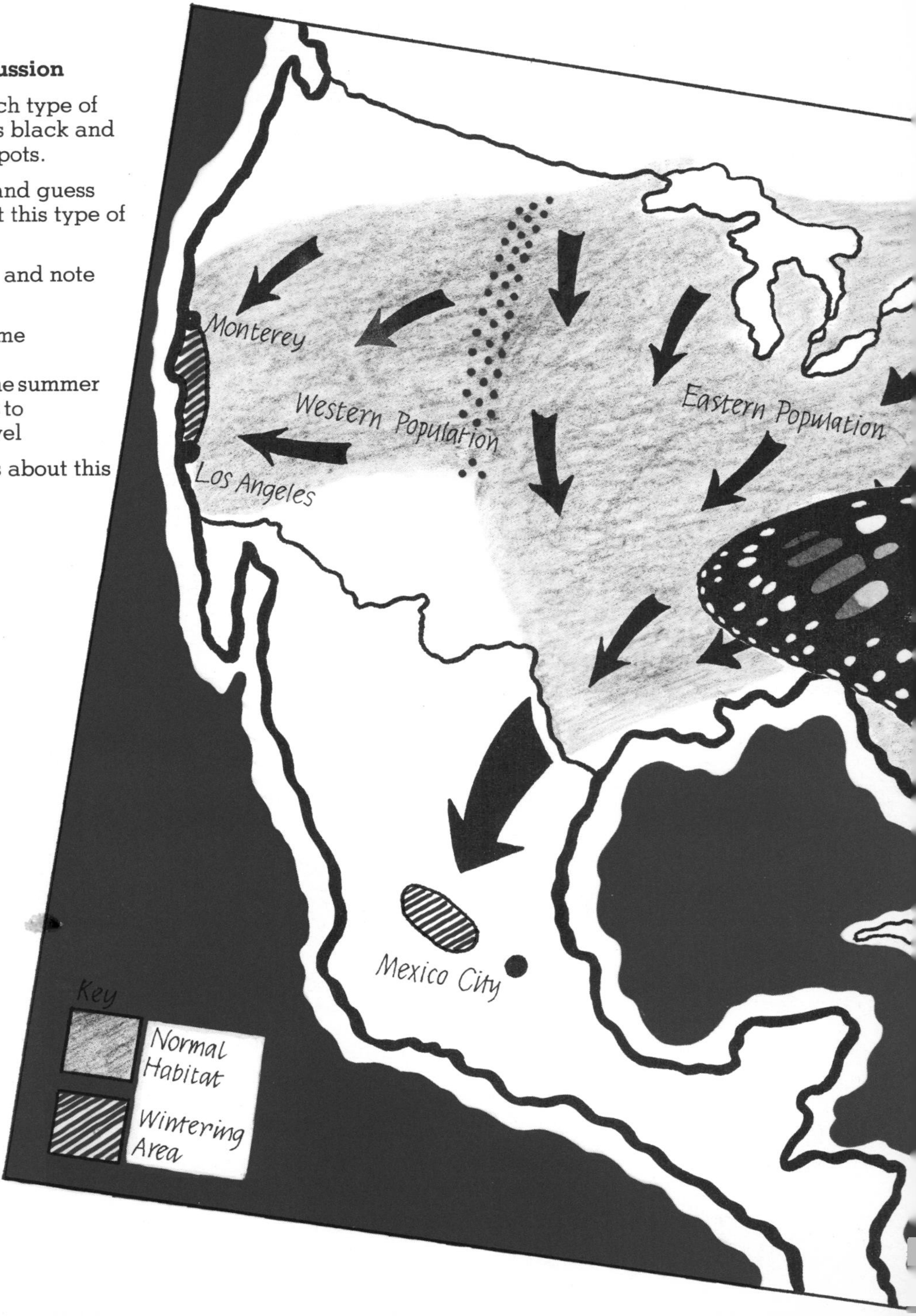

Monterey

Western Population

Eastern Population

Los Angeles

Mexico City

Key

Normal Habitat

Wintering Area

B Group game

Let's see how much you know about nature. Discuss these statements, and decide whether they are true.

Honeybees
1 The queen bee can lay more than 2,000 eggs per day.
2 The queen bee lives for 2 years.
3 Bees have 4 legs and 6 wings.

Spiders
1 Not all spiders make webs to catch their prey.
2 One species of spider lives under water.
3 Spiders have 8 legs.

Ants
1 Ants have good vision.
2 Some ants use other ants as slaves.
3 Some ants carry leaves on their heads.

When you have finished, tell the class which ones you think are true; also say which ones you think are false and why. Then check your answers with the teacher.

C Group discussion

1 Find out if your group is interested in nature, whether they read nature books or watch nature programmes. Do they, for example, know the names of common birds, flowers, and trees?

2 Some people think it's important to be close to nature. What do you think? Say how often you visit parks or go to the country.

migrate to	It's unbelievable!
live for	Incredible!
arrow	How interesting!
wings	I don't believe it!
journey	It can't be true!
insects	

3 A strange incident

A Open class discussion

1 Funny things are always happening to people. One day, a very funny thing happened to Lyn Donovan, the girl in the photograph. The photograph was taken immediately after the incident. Look at it and try to imagine what happened.

2 On the tape is an account of the whole story. Listen to it and note down:

what Lyn was doing_____
what she saw _____
how she felt _____
what the old lady was doing _____

3 Now say exactly what happened.

B Role playing—in groups of 4

Roles: *Lyn Donovan*
Driver of the car behind
Policeman
Witness

Imagine and act out the conversation which took place after the accident. Begin like this:

Policeman — Hello. What happened here?
Lyn — Well, I was driving along the road when I saw ....

C Group discussion

Has anything funny (ie amusing or strange) ever happened to you, your friends, or your family? Tell your group about it.

witness	run over
crash into	look for
false teeth	I don't believe it
on your hands	It's true
and knees	Well, I never
shocked	How strange
surprised	Good heavens
frightened	

4 Talk about your country

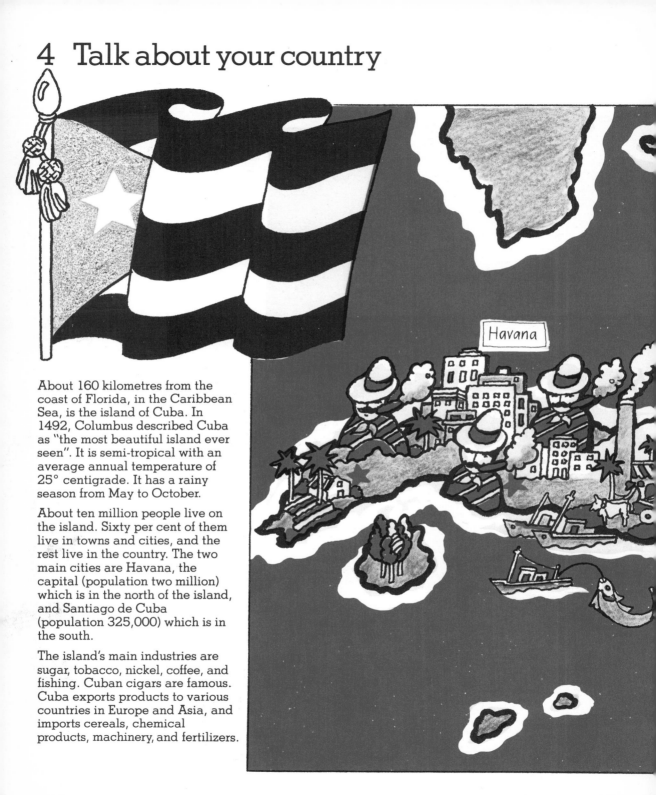

About 160 kilometres from the coast of Florida, in the Caribbean Sea, is the island of Cuba. In 1492, Columbus described Cuba as "the most beautiful island ever seen". It is semi-tropical with an average annual temperature of 25° centigrade. It has a rainy season from May to October.

About ten million people live on the island. Sixty per cent of them live in towns and cities, and the rest live in the country. The two main cities are Havana, the capital (population two million) which is in the north of the island, and Santiago de Cuba (population 325,000) which is in the south.

The island's main industries are sugar, tobacco, nickel, coffee, and fishing. Cuban cigars are famous. Cuba exports products to various countries in Europe and Asia, and imports cereals, chemical products, machinery, and fertilizers.

A Open class discussion

1 Read the text and find out if your classmates understood it by asking such questions as:

> How many people live in towns and cities?
> How many people live in the country?
> What did Columbus say about Cuba? etc.

2 Look at the map and identify the countries which are near Cuba.

3 On the tape is a short report on Cuban education. Listen to it, and say what is unusual about this educational system.

B Group discussion

Now talk about your country.

1 Say what the population is, how many people live in the country, and how many people live in the towns and cities.

2 Say what your country produces, and who you export the products to.

3 What does your country import? From where?

4 Talk about the differences between education in Cuba and education in your country.

dairy products	water
wheat	harvest the crops
rice	I don't know much
corn	about . . .
textiles	That's not true
steel	approximately
petroleum	round about
plant	more or less
weed	

5 Mrs Warner takes to the road

A Open class discussion

1 Look at the illustration and describe the scene.

2 Mr and Mrs Warner, the couple in the illustration, are talking to a car salesman. Listen to their conversation on the tape and then compare the cars mentioned for size, comfort, price, and so on.

3 Say which car Mrs Warner wants and give the reasons for her choice. How does Mr Warner feel about this?

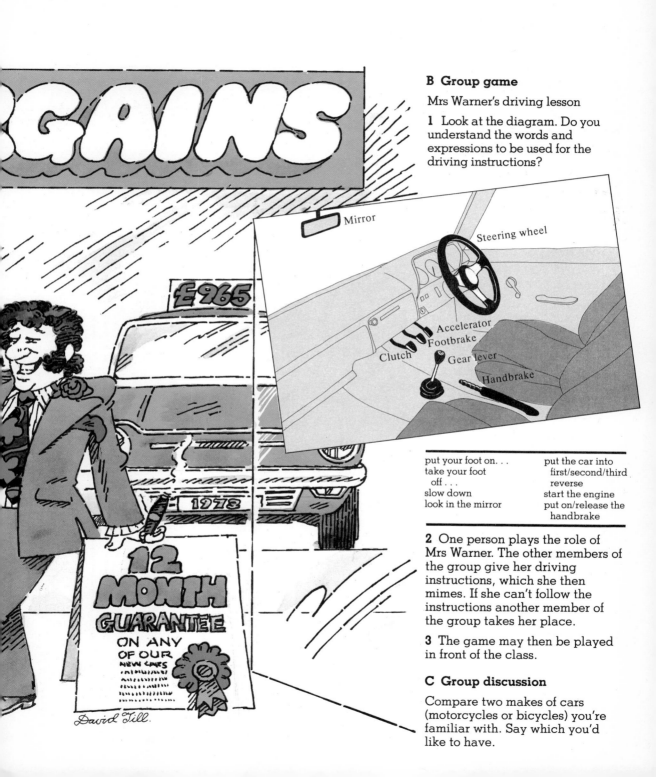

B Group game

Mrs Warner's driving lesson

1 Look at the diagram. Do you understand the words and expressions to be used for the driving instructions?

Mirror

Steering wheel

Accelerator

Footbrake

Clutch

Gear lever

Handbrake

put your foot on...	put the car into first/second/third reverse
take your foot off...	
slow down	start the engine
look in the mirror	put on/release the handbrake

2 One person plays the role of Mrs Warner. The other members of the group give her driving instructions, which she then mimes. If she can't follow the instructions another member of the group takes her place.

3 The game may then be played in front of the class.

C Group discussion

Compare two makes of cars (motorcycles or bicycles) you're familiar with. Say which you'd like to have.

6 Record breakers

A Open class discussion

1 Look at the photograph of Robert Wadlow and guess how tall he was.

2 Listen to the tape and note down these interesting details about Robert Wadlow:

Birth weight _____
Weight at a year _____
Weight at 22 _____
Height at 22 _____
Shoe size _____

3 Now talk about Wadlow. Compare him to the average man.

4 How was Wadlow's life different from yours? Consider the trouble he had with spaces such as rooms and doors; also furniture and clothes. Imagine what happened when he went to the cinema or a party. Think of other problems he had.

Robert Wadlow — history's tallest ever human

B Group game

Robert Wadlow is the tallest man ever recorded. In what way are the following "record breakers"?

a The Nile
b The Concorde
c La Paz (capital of Bolivia)
d Angel Falls, Venezuela
e Mount Everest
f Caspian Sea
g The Louisiana Superdome
h Sears Tower, Chicago

Now check your answers with the rest of the class to see if they agree.

C Group discussion

In the group game we discussed world records. Now let's go on to national records. Tell your group about record breakers in your country. Consider:

rivers	cities
mountains	buildings
lakes	sportsmen, etc.

special	too
normal	nearly
abnormal	I suppose
bend	I agree/don't agree
hit one's head	I haven't the
make fun of	faintest idea
enough	

7 What's on?

A Open class discussion

As you see in the illustration, Henry is looking at the newspaper. He and Sally are trying to decide which film to see. Listen to their conversation on the tape, and say:

- which films Henry mentions
- which film Sally decides to see
- why she chooses it
- why she doesn't want to see the others
- whether Henry is happy with her choice

PLAZA 1
OFF
LEICESTER SQUARE
437 1616

FUNNY GIRL

Barbara Streisand,
James Caan, Omar Sharif
Director
Herbert Ross
A musical for all the family

5.00 7.30 10.00

PLAZA 2

RYAN O'NEAL
AND
ALI McGRAW
IN

DIRECTOR: ARTHUR HILLER
The most moving film of the century

5.30 8.00 10.30

LYRIC
UNION STREET
723 4849

COMEDY

ANNIE HALL

With DIANE KEATON
WOODY ALLEN

Director: WOODY ALLEN
Four Oscars

5.00 8.00

6.30 8.30

Queen Street

SCENES FROM A MARRIAGE

LIV ULLMANN   BIBI ANDERSO
DIRECTOR: INGMAR BERGMA
A psychological drama

Late show every night 10.45

odeon

Retained for 6th week

RIGHTMARE

RT DAVIS DEBORAH FAIRFAX
DIRECTOR
PETER WALKER

Horror all the way!
ADULTS ONLY
Sunday 5.45 8.15
Week 5.30 8.00 10.30

CINE CENTRE
Tollcross
Now showing: 5.00 7.30 10.00

BROKEN ARROW

JAMES STEWART
JEFF CHANDLER
DEBRA PAGET

DIRECTOR:
DELMER DAVES

A great western

Programme may be subject to late change.

IMPERIAL
PICCADILLY

A BRIDGE TOO FAR

ll star cast—Dirk Bogarde,
ean Connery, Gene Hackman,
aurence Olivier, etc.
irector: Richard Attenborough
A war film

Daily 7.00 10.00

CURZON
HAYMARKET

5.00 7.30 10.00

JAWS

RICHARD DREYFUSS
ROY SCHEIDER LORRAINE GARY
DIRECTOR:
STEVEN SPIELBERG

ADULTS ONLY.

Action and suspense

ROYAL
437 1501

5.15 7.15 9.15

CLOSE NCOUNTERS
OF THE THIRD KIND

WITH RICHARD DREYFUSS
FRANCOIS TRUFFAUT
RECTOR: STEVEN SPIELBERG.
FOR ALL THE FAMILY

RITZ
4.30   QUEEN STREET   8.00

Gone With The Wind

WITH
CLARK GABLE,
VIVIEN LEIGH, LESLIE HOWARD
DIRECTOR:
VICTOR FLEMING
Romance and passion

B Role playing — in pairs

Choose from these roles: parent
and child; aunt and niece or
nephew; host and overseas visitor;
two friends; husband and wife.

Now imagine you're going to the
cinema tonight. Look to see what's
on, and try to decide on a film.

C Group discussion

1 Talk about the best film you've
seen recently. What was it about?

2 Who is your favourite actor,
actress, and director? Say why.

romantic	comedy
violent	musical
intellectual	horror film
commercial	It's on at . . .
funny	Who's in it?
frightening	What about . . . ?
entertaining	What else . . . ?
western	I can't stand . . .
adventure story	Get a move on
love story	appeal to
war film	

8 Wild life in danger

A Open class discussion

1 This table gives information about four species of wild life in danger of extinction. It doesn't say what the tusks, oil, and skins are used for or made into. Discuss this, and then put the information in the appropriate box.

2 Listen to the tape about these endangered species, and at the same time check your information.

3 Say whether you are interested in wild life, and what you feel about the disappearance of these species. Do you think it's necessary for man to hunt these animals?

B Group discussion

1 What other wild animals are hunted by man? Say where they are found and why they are hunted.

2 Think of your possessions, and say what you have that's made from a part of an animal.

3 The only chance most of us have to see wild animals is when we go to zoos. Do you think it's true that animals suffer in zoos and, if so, in what way? Describe what you've seen in zoos.

SPECIES	FOUND IN	HUNTED FOR	USED FOR/ MADE INTO	POPULA-TION
AFRICAN ELEPHANT	Africa	Tusks		Rapidly decreasing
BLUE WHALE	Antarctic	Oil		13,000
INDIAN CROCODILE	India, Sri Lanka, Burma	Skin		Very few left
HARP SEAL	Arctic/ Gulf of St. Lawrence	Oil (Adults) White skins (Pups)		Decreasing

cosmetics	killed
lubricants	clubbed
ivory	caught
fur coat	poisoned
rug	It's a pity
jewellery	It's a shame
ornaments	It's terrible
cage	It's necessary
shot	

9 It's here to stay

A Open class discussion

1 Say what the people in the cartoon are doing. How does the woman who is speaking feel, and why does she feel this way?

2 Alongside the cartoon it says that TV is good for you because it stimulates your mind, and you can see the news on it. Add any other reasons you can think of and tell the class about them.

3 Listen to the tape, and write down why TV is bad, especially for children.

TV is good for you because:

1. It stimulates your mind.
2. You can see the news on it.

_____

_____

TV is bad because:

_____

_____

_____

_____

_____

Now tell the class what the letter said.

educational	entertaining
programmes	relaxing
commercials	creative
advertising	funny
documentaries	I quite agree
choose	Do you agree
select	with . . . ?
exaggerate	What do you
turn on/off	think?

"There's no doubt about it, there are times when TV incites me to violence."

B Group discussion

1 Ask your group if they agree with the complaints about TV made in the letter, and give your own opinion. Is the solution to get rid of your set?

2 Talk about the programmes you watch on TV and say why you like them. Discuss other things you enjoy doing in your spare time.

10 What are you afraid of?

A Open class discussion

1 "What are you most afraid of?" a team of researchers asked 3,000 U.S. inhabitants. The fears are listed below, and on the tape is a report of the study. Listen to the tape and note down the results— that is the percentage—alongside each fear.

2 Don't you find the results surprising? For example: isn't it strange that more people are afraid of speaking in front of a group than financial problems, or death? Discuss the other results in the table.

3 According to the survey, women are more fearful than men. Which fears do you think men named most, and which do you think women named most? Give your reasons.

%	Fear
	Speaking in front of a group
	Heights
	Insects and bugs
	Financial problems
	Deep water
	Sickness
	Death
	Flying
	Loneliness
	Dogs
	Driving—riding in a car
	The dark
	Lifts (elevators)
	Escalators

B Group discussion

1 Say whether the fears in the table are also your fears.

2 The people in the pictures are obviously petrified. What are they afraid of? Have you ever felt as frightened as this? If so, tell the group about the occasion.

3 Fortunately, there's much more happiness in life than fear. Talk about some of your happiest moments.

I can't stand	I remember when
I'm terrified of	How terrible!
I'm frightened of	both
I'm afraid of	once
I was petrified	

11 Should children go to school?

The Kirkbride family live in a large, three hundred year-old house in Norfolk. They are an unusual family. John and Melinda Kirkbride do not send their children to school. And they do not believe in teaching them at home, either. James, 18, Tamara, 15, Tigger, 14, and Hoppy, 10, have spent the last four years doing what other children enjoy only at weekends and holidays. They get up when they like, and spend the day doing what they want. They walk, swim, fish, paint, read, play musical instruments, perform their own plays, cook, or just sit around and talk.

John and Melinda Kirkbride took their children out of the local school in 1973. It was quite easy to persuade the local education authorities to let them do this, because John is a trained teacher. But, says John, "*teach* is a swear word in this house. It destroys the child's natural talent and creativity. Now, *learning*—that's different. All our children learn when and if they want to learn something. They look it up in books or they ask someone who knows. They use their initiative— which is more than any school can teach them. Examinations are the worst part of the educational system. They produce a fear of failure, a lack of confidence, and a lack of individuality."

A Open class discussion

1 Read the passage and tell the class about the Kirkbride family. Say why they don't send their children to school.

2 Describe the kind of school you think John and Melinda would like to send their children to.

3 On the tape is a conversation between two young people who have just left school. Listen to it, and then talk about their attitude to school.

B Group discussion

1 Talk about the subjects you're studying/you studied at school. Which of them are useful?

2 Discuss other benefits from school apart from learning. For example: making friends, playing games, etc.

3 Here's a fairly typical British secondary school curriculum. Say which subjects the students must study, and which they don't have to.

☐ Art
☐ Art History
■ Biology
■ Chemistry
☐ Domestic science
■ English language
■ English literature
■ Foreign language (French, German or Spanish)
■ Geography
■ History
☐ Latin
☐ Music
■ Mathematics
■ Physical education
■ Physics
☐ Religion
☐ Woodwork

Key: *Obligatory* ■ *Optional* ☐

4 Say which subjects you think should be included in a modern curriculum. For instance, should children study ecology, current affairs, social problems, human relations, marriage skills, child care, etc.?

depend on	training
take/pass/fail an	career
exam	It's very important
interested in	Don't you think so?
leave school	I must say I don't
go in for	agree
subject	It's very useful
discipline	

12 Trouble at work

A Open class discussion

1 The photograph shows Mr Miles in his office with his new secretary, Jennifer Jones. Describe the scene.

2 Mr Miles was impressed with Jennifer when he interviewed her. He thought she would be a good secretary. However, now that he has seen her work, he isn't happy with her. Listen to the conversation on the tape, and say why.

punctual	leave early
inefficient	She/he's hopeless
harrassed	on top of
middle aged	everything
come late	I'm terribly/awfully
clumsy	sorry
do your best	I'm afraid . . .

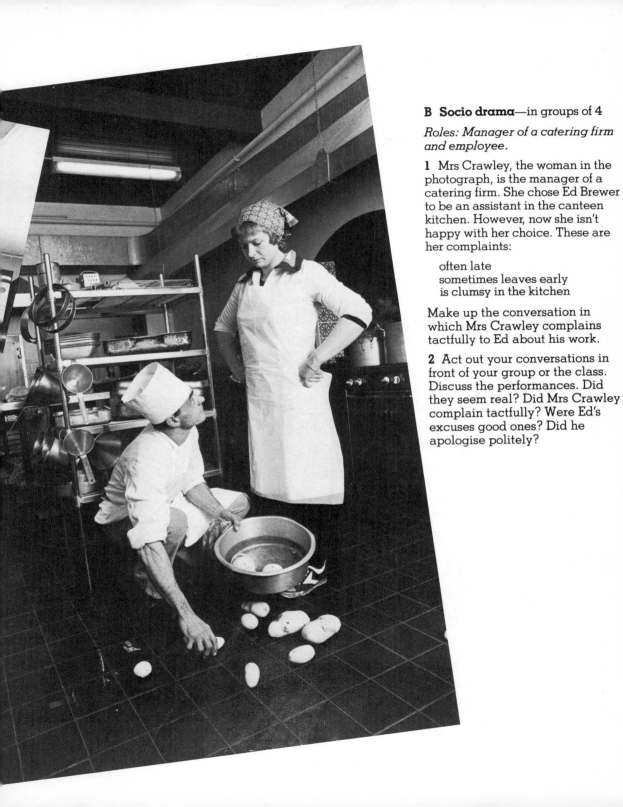

B Socio drama—in groups of 4

Roles: Manager of a catering firm and employee.

1 Mrs Crawley, the woman in the photograph, is the manager of a catering firm. She chose Ed Brewer to be an assistant in the canteen kitchen. However, now she isn't happy with her choice. These are her complaints:

> often late
> sometimes leaves early
> is clumsy in the kitchen

Make up the conversation in which Mrs Crawley complains tactfully to Ed about his work.

2 Act out your conversations in front of your group or the class. Discuss the performances. Did they seem real? Did Mrs Crawley complain tactfully? Were Ed's excuses good ones? Did he apologise politely?

13 Let's have a party

A Open class discussion

1 Look at the cartoon—is it funny? Say what is happening, and what the various members of the household are doing.

2 On the tape is a conversation between Maggie, her friend Cindy, and Maggie's parents. Maggie and Cindy are planning a party. Say what their plans are, and how Maggie's parents feel about the party. What are their objections?

3 Is there any trouble in your house when someone wants to have a party?

soft drinks	tired
beer	worried
fruit punch	horrified
cheese dip	Oh, no!
crisps	Not another!
peanuts	Come in
guitar	I hope I'm not
cassettes	disturbing you
record player	Leave them to it
loud speakers	Oh well
busy	Don't worry

"I'm having a last-bank-holiday-of-the-fortnight party — bring Harry, Georgie, Dickie, Punghi, Ronnie, Wilmer and the gang, and ask Buggsie to bring his drums and hi-fi with him."

B Socio drama — in groups of 4

Planning a party
*Roles: Mother, father, teenage son/
daughter, and friend.*

1 The teenager and friend should
set a date and time and make a
list of guests and things needed
for the party in the boxes
provided below. The parents can
make a list of their objections.

DATE
PLACE
FOOD
DRINK
MUSIC

Objections

2 Using the information you have
written down, make up and
rehearse a conversation similar to
the one on tape.

3 Act out the conversations in
front of the class. Discuss the
performances. Say whether they
seemed real and whether the
language was natural.

14 Too good to be true

A Open class discussion

1 Read the file cards and then describe the different islands. Say where they are and how much they cost.

2 Compare the islands and say whether you think any of them are a good buy.

3 All of these islands sound marvellous. However, some may have problems that are not obvious from the details here. What problems might there be?

4 Listen to the conversation on the tape between a millionaire and his wife talking about Coconut Island. Say what the good features of the island are, and what the millionaire will do if he buys it. How does his wife feel about it?

B Group game

1 Pretend you have come into a large fortune and are about to buy one of the islands advertised. Choose one, and note down the features you like about it.

2 Speculate on what you will do with the island if you buy it. Find out what the other members of your group will do with the ones they have chosen.

3 Pretend you meet again ten years after buying the island. Tell your group about your success or misfortune. For example:

Was your island a good choice?
Did you do all you planned to do? If not, why not?
Do you still own the island? etc.

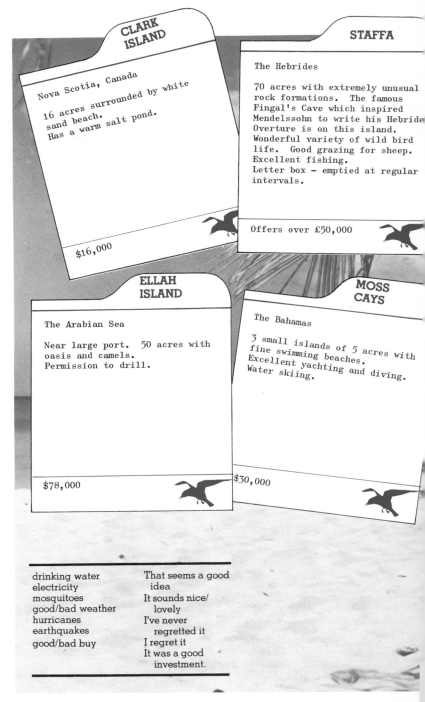

CLARK ISLAND

Nova Scotia, Canada

16 acres surrounded by white sand beach.
Has a warm salt pond.

$16,000

STAFFA

The Hebrides

70 acres with extremely unusual rock formations. The famous Fingal's Cave which inspired Mendelssohn to write his Hebrides Overture is on this island.
Wonderful variety of wild bird life. Good grazing for sheep.
Excellent fishing.
Letter box – emptied at regular intervals.

Offers over £50,000

ELLAH ISLAND

The Arabian Sea

Near large port. 50 acres with oasis and camels.
Permission to drill.

$78,000

MOSS CAYS

The Bahamas

3 small islands of 5 acres with fine swimming beaches.
Excellent yachting and diving.
Water skiing.

$30,000

drinking water
electricity
mosquitoes
good/bad weather
hurricanes
earthquakes
good/bad buy

That seems a good idea
It sounds nice/ lovely
I've never regretted it
I regret it
It was a good investment.

PALMYRA ISLANDS

South of Hawaii

1,200 acres with giant (30 metre high) coconut palms. Has an air-strip large enough to land a 727 jet.

4,000.000

CANDY ISLAND

rida, Gulf of Mexico

cres with fertile soil and ge cedar trees. Good fishing.

$110,000

15 A historic city

A Open class discussion

1 Look at the photographs. Do you know what city this is, and which country it's in? Say what's unusual about the men's clothes. Which musical instruments do they have?

2 Listen to the conversation on the tape between two strangers in a pub, and note down:

> where Nelson Brammer
>   is from _____
> how long he's staying
>   in Edinburgh _____
> what the Royal Mile is _____
> when Scotland was united
>   with England _____
> which famous Queen lived in
>   Holyrood Palace _____
> what Rory tells Nelson
>   to buy _____

3 Now tell the class about Nelson Brammer and other details you noted down.

4 If you have been to Scotland, tell the class about your visit.

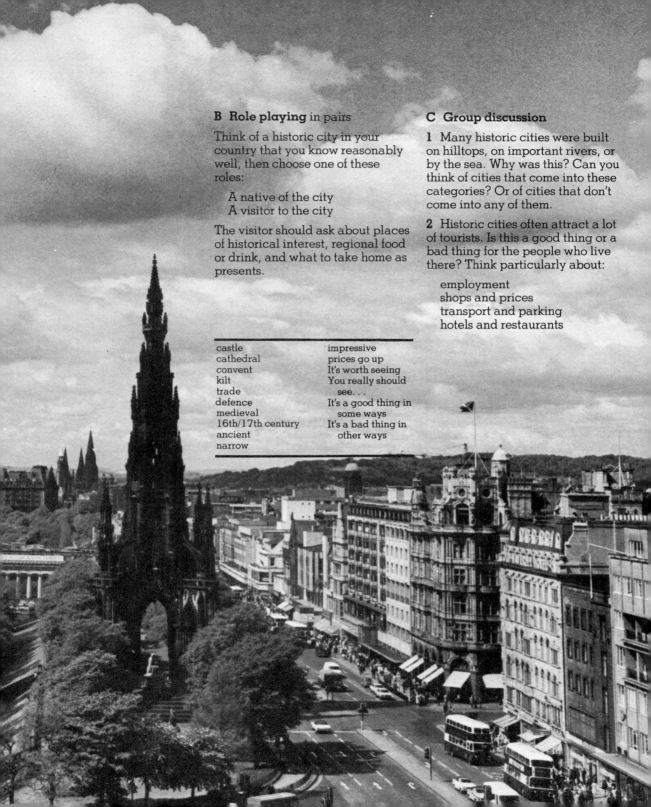

B Role playing in pairs

Think of a historic city in your country that you know reasonably well, then choose one of these roles:

    A native of the city
    A visitor to the city

The visitor should ask about places of historical interest, regional food or drink, and what to take home as presents.

castle	impressive
cathedral	prices go up
convent	It's worth seeing
kilt	You really should
trade	see. . .
defence	It's a good thing in
medieval	some ways
16th/17th century	It's a bad thing in
ancient	other ways
narrow	

C Group discussion

1 Many historic cities were built on hilltops, on important rivers, or by the sea. Why was this? Can you think of cities that come into these categories? Or of cities that don't come into any of them.

2 Historic cities often attract a lot of tourists. Is this a good thing or a bad thing for the people who live there? Think particularly about:

    employment
    shops and prices
    transport and parking
    hotels and restaurants

16 A helping hand

A Open class discussion

1 Describe the scene in the photograph.

2 Listen to the tape and fill in the missing parts of the conversation between Jean, Simon, and Helen.

Simon Hello. Having trouble with the typewriter?

Jean Yes. There's something wrong with it.

Helen _____

Jean That's kind of you. I don't now much about typewriters.

Simon Have you plugged it in?

Jean _____

Helen Have you switched it on?

Jean _____.

Simon Have you cleaned it recently?

Jean Mm . . . _____

Simon You should clean it more often, you know.

Jean _____

Simon Well, I can't see anything wrong with it.

Jean Oh dear. _____ technician then.

Helen Hold on. I see what's wrong.

Jean _____?

Helen It's the plug. There's a wire loose.

Jean Oh, _____!

Helen I'll repair it for you, if you have a screwdriver.

Jean _____
I'll get the screwdriver.

3 Say what's wrong with the typewriter and whether Simon and Helen can help.

B Socio drama—in groups of 6

Roles: Driver of broken down car and two people who have stopped to help.

1 Imagine and make up the conversation between the driver of the broken down car and the two people who have stopped to help.

Here are some things that could be checked to find the reason for the breakdown:

    petrol
    oil
    water
    battery
    plugs
    fan belt
    carburettor

2 Act out your conversation in front of your group or class.

3 Discuss the performances. Was the help offered naturally? Did the driver sound grateful?

C Group discussion

Talk about an incident where you (or someone you know) either gave or received a helping hand.

look at	Can I help you?
check	I'm very
engine	grateful . . .
mechanic	

17 How's your general knowledge?

A Open class discussion

1 Do you know who the man in the photograph is? Listen to the tape which gives information about his life, and then tell the class about him.

2 Talk about ways of communicating before the invention of the telephone. How did news travel? How did people get in touch with one another?

3 Do you have a telephone? If so, do you feel that life would be better in your house without it?

B General knowledge quiz

Work in pairs, and decide what the following are famous for. Then fill in the answers.

1 Lee Harvey Oswald was the man. . . .

2 Anne Frank was the girl. . . .

3 Alexander Fleming. . . .

4 Marco Polo. . . .

5 Johann Gutenberg. . . .

6 Nadia Comaneci. . . .

7 The Titanic was the ship. . . .

8 The Hindenburg. . . .

9 Vesuvius. . . .

10 Bethlehem is the place. . . .

11 The Bermuda Triangle. . . .

12 Fort Knox. . . .

When you've finished, read your answers to the class to see if they agree with them. If no-one has finished in 10 minutes, the pair with the most correct answers will be the winners.

C Group discussion

Bell and Gutenberg were inventors whose inventions greatly changed people's lives. Ask your group what they think the most important inventions of this century are, and why. Say what you think.

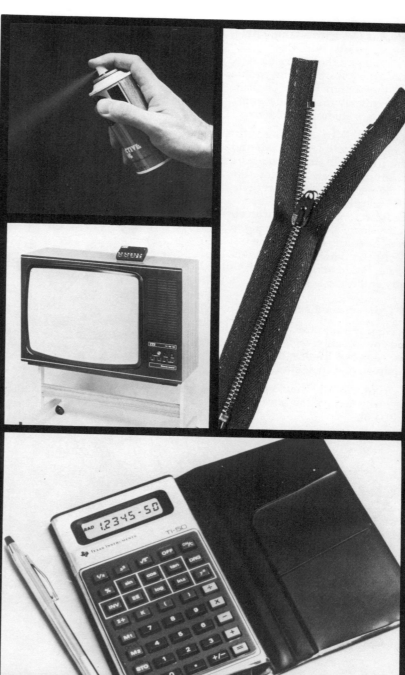

assassinate
discover
sink
erupt
explode

I couldn't live
without . . .
I can't remember
The name rings a
bell
I haven't a clue

18 Getting out of it

In England, many overseas students live with a family as paying guests. With this arrangement they learn more about the customs of the people, and they improve their English more quickly than if they were living in a students' residence.

Pedro and Niko are living with a family in North London: Mr and Mrs Trimm and their son, Andrew. In return for their kindness, the Trimms sometimes expect their student guests, and of course Andrew, to give a hand with some of the domestic maintenance jobs, such as spring-cleaning the kitchen or painting the garden fence. Pedro and Niko are usually very willing to help.

A Open class discussion

1 After reading the text, listen to the conversation on the tape between the Trimms, their son Andrew, and their student guests.

2 What was Mr Trimm's problem? Say why none of the boys could help him.

B Socio drama — in family size groups

Roles: father, mother and young people

1 The parents should choose a task while the young people choose, or think up, excuses for the weekend—Saturday and Sunday. The group should then work out the conversation.

Tasks
① clean out the garage
② paint the kitchen
③ wash the curtains
④ cut the grass
⑤ clean the refrigerator
⑥ wash the car

EXCUSES
date with a boyfriend
appointment with hairdresser
buy clothes
go to exhibition
meditate

2 Act out the conversation in front of the class, and discuss the performances. Were the excuses convincing?

I'm awfully sorry	What about Sunday?
I'm afraid I can't	That's too bad
I can't possibly	Oh well

19 Making a date

Making a date on the phone can be difficult, especially if you don't know the person (or the language) very well. Aldo, an Italian engineering student, tried to make a date with Sheila, a rather sensitive ballet student.

A Open class discussion

1 Listen to the tape of the conversation between Aldo and Sheila. Say what happened, what went wrong, and why Sheila didn't go out with Aldo. Did she *really* have something else to do . . .?

2 Listen to the tape of the conversation between Luigi and Sheila and discuss why it was better than the other.

B Socio drama—in groups of 4

Two people making a date

1 Choose one of the ideas for dates and prepare the telephone conversation with your partner.

2 Act out your dialogue in front of the group, or the class.

3 Discuss the performances. Which was the best? Why? Were they polite? Did they say the right things?

polite	go out with
rude	I'd love to
tactful/tactless	I'm afraid
say the right thing	I suppose/don't
say the wrong	suppose
thing	I hope
would you like	Of course
to . . .?	See you later

Ideas for dates

a You met on the train to Stratford on the way to a Shakespeare Festival. Call, and make a date for the theatre.

b You met at a party and talked about films. Call, and make a date for the cinema or another party.

c You met at an exhibition—you liked the same works. Phone, and invite your partner to another exhibition.

STATION

20 Let your body speak

A Open class discussion

1 Describe the people in the photographs and say what they're doing. What feelings are they trying to show with their gestures?

2 Listen to the conversation between Stephen and his friend George and then explain the trouble Stephen had with the hotel receptionist. Also say what gestures you think Stephen made when he wanted something to eat or drink, and when he didn't understand what people were saying.

This is what Stephen did to show he had toothache

B Group discussion

Most people scratch their heads when they're thinking. Do you do this? Think of all the gestures you usually make. Show them to your group and explain what they mean.

C Group game

1 Imagine you're talking to some friends and try to convey two of these feelings to them through gesture. The other members of the group should try to guess which feelings they are.

fear	disgust
anger	embarrassment
disagreement	happiness
determination	sadness

2 Imagine you're sitting in a train. Without using words, show the following:

a that you don't want anyone to sit next to you
b that you'd welcome company
c that you're tired of making the same journey every day

Now discuss each other's performances and say whether the message was clear.

welcome	stick your tongue
greet	out
insult	friendship
threaten	victory
shake hands	anger
shake your fist	boredom
raise your arms	tiredness
shake/nod your head	

Oxford University Press, Walton Street, Oxford OX2 6DP

Oxford London Glasgow New York Toronto Melbourne Wellington
Kuala Lumpur Singapore Hong Kong Tokyo Delhi Bombay
Calcutta Madras Karachi Nairobi Dar Es Salaam Cape Town

ISBN 0 19 432216 5   (Student's book 1)
ISBN 0 19 432217 3   (Student's book 2)
ISBN 0 19 432218 1   (Student's book 3)
ISBN 0 19 432219 X   (Teacher's book)

First published 1980
Second impression 1981

Printed in Spain by Mateu Cromo Artes
Graficas S.A.